Fishing Off the Wharf

by Don Long

photographs by Karen Angus

LEARNING
MEDIA®

Dad and I love to go fishing together.

First thing on Saturday morning,
we drive around to the rocks
to get mussels for bait.

Next we make some "chum"
for catching the herrings.
We open the mussels
over a bucket
to catch all the juice.

We mix in stale bread
and other scraps
that Dad has saved.

Then we drive to the wharf.

It's great fun down at the wharf.
There's always something happening.

A lot of people go there to fish.
We say "Hi!" to our friends.

First, we bait our hooks
with tiny bits of mussel.

8

Then we flick out some chum...
and the herrings go mad.
All you have to do
is throw in your line
and you'll catch lots.

9

As soon as we've got about
twenty fish, that's it.
We can't eat more than that.
We pack up and head for home.

We carry the herrings home
in a bucket of sea water to keep them fresh.
Dad always moans when the water slops
onto the floor of the car.
I just say,
"We should get a bucket with a lid!"

Dad scrapes off the scales,
then guts the fish.
He slices them open
and pulls out the insides.
I'm glad I don't have to do that!

The cat loves it
when we bring herrings home.

There's nothing better than
herrings and French fries.
We cook the French fries in the oven,
and fry the herrings in a big pan.

Dad gives me half,
but he always ends up finishing mine.
He says that when I get older,
we should buy a boat.
But I think the wharves are just fine.

Catching Herrings

Making a Fishing Line

If you want to try fishing for herrings, you could make your own handline.
You will need:
- a short piece of wood, as thick as a broom handle
- some light nylon fishing line (enough to reach right down into the water)
- a cork
- some *very* small hooks.

1. Tie one end of the line to the piece of wood, and the other end to the cork.	2. Near the cork, make three or four loops in the line, like this.	3. Tie one hook onto each of the loops.

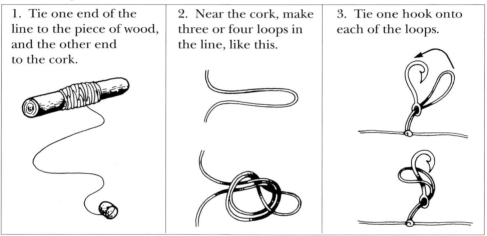

When you aren't using the handline, put pieces of cork on the tips of the hooks.
They are very sharp.

Bait and Chum

You can use mussel meat for bait. Put a small piece onto each hook.
To make the chum, you could mix stale bread with chopped-up bits of mussel or fishy cat food.
Flick out some chum, and the herrings will come up to eat it. Throw in your line, and see what you can catch.
Don't go fishing by yourself. Always go with an older friend or relation. They could help you to cut up the mussels and bait the hooks.